DRUGS AND YOUR BROTHERS AND SISTERS

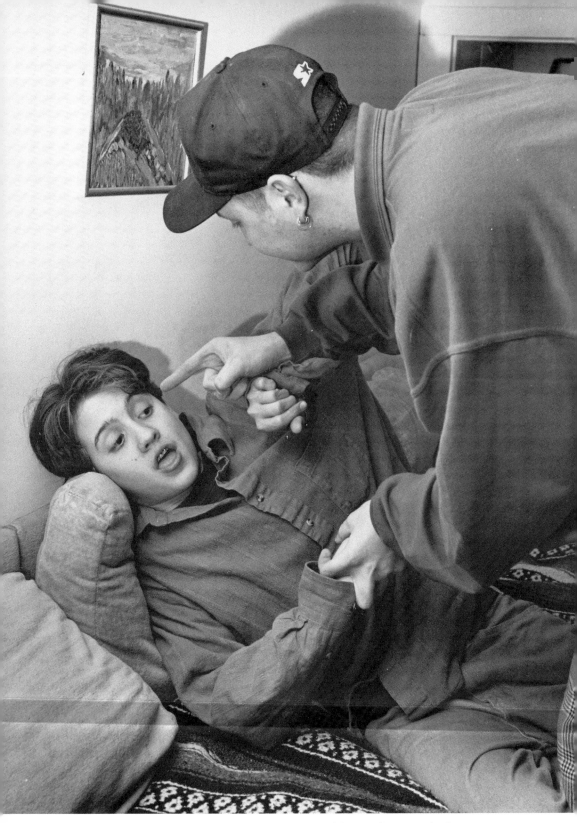

Brothers and sisters sometimes come to blows when one finds
out that the other is into drugs.

THE DRUG ABUSE PREVENTION LIBRARY

DRUGS AND YOUR BROTHERS AND SISTERS

Rhoda McFarland

THE ROSEN PUBLISHING GROUP, INC.

NEW YORK

Published in 1992 by The Rosen Publishing Group, Inc.
29 East 21st Street, New York, NY 10010

First Edition

Printed in Canada

*The people pictured in this book are only models; they, in no way,
practice or endorse the activities illustrated. Captions serve only to
explain the subjects of photographs and do not in any way imply a
connection between the real-life models and the staged situations
shown.*

Library of Congress Cataloging-in-Publication Data
McFarland, Rhoda.
        Drugs and your brothers and sisters/by Rhoda
        McFarland. —1st ed.
        (The Drug Abuse Prevention Library)
        Includes bibliographical references and index.
        Summary: Discusses the effect of drug abuse on the
        family, particularly siblings, of the abuser and what
        family members can do to help each other.
                ISBN 0-8239-1266-3
                1. Teenagers—United States—Drug abuse—
                Juvenile literature. 2. Narcotic addicts—
                United States—Family relationships—Juvenile
                literature. 3. Drug abuse—United States—
                Prevention—Juvenile literature. 4. Brothers
                and sisters—United States—Juvenile literature.
                [1. Drug abuse. 2. Family problems.
                3. Brothers and sisters.] I. Title. II. Series.
                HV5824. Y68M39 1991
                362.29'132—dc20   90–49277
                                                            CIP
                                                            AC

Contents

An early effect of growing drug involvement is loss of pride in your appearance.

CHAPTER 1

What Is Drug Addiction?

*L*isa slammed her bedroom door. She stuck the desk chair under the doorknob the way they do in the movies. Then she sat on the floor with her back against the door and cried. That monster wasn't her brother. Yelling and cursing were one thing. Chasing her with a knife was something else. Rob wanted to kill her. She saw it in his eyes. He was crazy. He was never like this until he started using drugs. "My brother is a drug addict. Rob is a drug addict." Lisa said the words slowly to herself. Hugging her knees and rocking with pain, she cried.

8 | *What Is Drug Addiction?*

In a way, Rob *is* out of his mind. His brain is not working right because of his drug use. What is happening to him?

Rob is a very sick young man. He is not evil or weak. He does not just have a bad habit. He has a disease—the disease of *chemical dependence.*

Chemical dependence has symptoms like any other disease. People who have it don't know it. They won't admit it. That *denial* is a symptom of the disease. Rob used to get buzzed on a couple of beers. Now he needs a six-pack to feel anything. Needing more of the drug to get the feeling he wants is called *tolerance.* It is a sign of growing dependence.

Without drugs, Rob breaks out in sweats and feels sick to his stomach. He has a *physical dependence* on drugs. His body needs them. His mind tells him that he must have drugs. That is *psychological dependence.* His psychological dependence makes him want the drug no matter what it takes to get it. He will lie or steal or hurt others. The *compulsion* to use is so great that he must do it again and again. He has no control over how much he uses or what happens when he uses. When Rob starts using, he doesn't know when he will stop.

That is what *addiction* is all about. It is the compulsion to use a drug. It is the loss of control over how much is used or how long it is used.

Some people think problems cause addiction. They say, "Just find the problem and the drinking will stop." Problems do not cause addiction. Addiction causes problems. Addiction *is* what is wrong.

Besides being the main problem, chemical dependence is *progressive.* It gets worse the longer drugs are used. The only way to stop it from getting worse is to stop drinking or using other drugs. It does not go away. In fact, addicts have the disease for the rest of their lives.

Even though the disease is permanent, it can be stopped. As long as any drug, including alcohol, is not used, the disease will not get worse. The person can learn to live a happy life without drugs.

Without help, the disease kills. Drug overdose and heart attack are common killers. Many addicts don't live long enough to die from the disease itself. They die from fights or accidents. The suicide rate is high among addicts. Many teen addicts cannot get treatment or are so far gone that no one will help them. Addiction kills unless the addict gets help.

10 | ## Who Becomes Addicted?

No one knows what causes addiction. No one knows why some people get the disease and others do not. Some important things *are* known. Chemical dependence runs in families. Studies have shown that the brain waves of sons of alcoholics are different from those whose fathers are not alcoholic. In 1990 scientists announced finding a gene for *alcoholism*. People with two alcoholic parents are 400 times more likely to become addicted to alcohol and other drugs. Those with one alcoholic parent are 35 times more likely to be alcoholic. Addiction in any family member— grandfather, uncle, aunt, brother, sister, cousin—is a warning that you are at high risk.

How Can You Tell If You Are Addicted?

It is not how often you drink or use other drugs. It is not how much you drink or use. It is what happens to you when you drink or use. Here are some questions you can ask yourself. If you answer yes they are signs that you may be in trouble with chemicals.

- Do you get into fights when you drink or use?

- Do your friends have to tell you what you did because you don't remember? That is called a *blackout.* It is a very serious warning sign that you are in trouble with chemicals.
- Do you say you will not get drunk and then do so?
- Have you ever felt sick while using but kept on using?
- Do you gulp down the first few drinks?
- Do you want an extra hit to get you going?
- Have your friends said you are drinking or using other drugs too much?
- Do you think about drinking or using?
- Do you talk a lot about partying?
- Have your grades been going down?
- Are you having more problems with your parents?
- Have you ever felt guilty about something you did when you were high?
- Do you lie about how much you use?
- Do you drink or use other drugs to forget your problems?
- Do you drink or use alone?

Yes answers to any of the questions means that chemicals are causing problems in your life. They are warning signs that you are becoming dependent.

A warning signal of drug or alcohol dependence is loss of interest in your room or prized possessions.

CHAPTER 2

How Did This Happen to My Brother/Sister?

As the tears rolled down her face, Lisa leaned her head back against the door. She was so confused. How did this happen? What made Rob start to use drugs anyway? Why would he do such a thing?

Why Do Teens Use Drugs?

Lisa did not know why Rob started using drugs. No one really knows the answer. There is no one reason that someone uses alcohol or other drugs. Young people give a number of reasons.

Rob and his buddies were bored. They didn't have much to do when they started drinking. It was exciting to do something they knew they should not do.

13

14 Most teens say that they think their friends won't like them if they don't join in smoking dope. *Peer pressure* is hard to resist. It is important to be liked and accepted by people your own age.

Some teens do not feel loved by their parents. They look for a group that will love and accept them. Users are always glad to welcome new users. Unhappy teens often find a group that accepts them and a chemical to make them feel good. It seems to be the answer to their problems.

Gary didn't like the way his parents treated him. They had all kinds of stupid rules. They punished him for nothing, he thought. Well, he showed them. Drugs were his way to get back at them.

During the teen years you are going through all kinds of changes. Many times you feel very unsure of yourself. Sometimes you feel hopeless. You may think you can't do anything right. At times you feel that no one likes you. You don't like yourself. When all of these feelings come together, you feel very *depressed*. That is when some teens use alcohol and other drugs to feel better.

Many teens are like Rob's friend, Jeff. Jeff's parents think it is very important to get a good education. They want Jeff to go to college and "make something of him-self." They push him to do better. Jeff feels that he is never good enough. He worries about failing. His fear is so great that on test days he feels sick. When Jeff gets high on marijuana, he doesn't have those terrible feelings.

Michelle's terrible feelings come from being so shy. She is sure that anything she says will be stupid. She feels that no one wants to be around her. She wishes she could be like other kids. Michelle has found that when she drinks, she loses those awful feelings of shyness. She can talk to people without being afraid. Alcohol helps her feel socially acceptable.

Some teens hear about getting high and wonder what it's like. They start using just because they are curious. Before they know it, they are hooked. Angela was like that. She knew lots of kids who got high on alcohol and other drugs. She wondered what it felt like to be high. One night she was at a party where there was a lot of beer and pot. The boy she was with brought her some beer. The girl she was sitting next to passed her a joint. "Well, why not?" she thought. "I just want to see what it's like. It's not as if I'm going to keep on doing it." But she did.

16   When Mike was small his father gave him sips of his beer. When Mike was twelve he and his father drank beer and watched the ball game together on TV. By then, Mike knew where his father kept a *stash* of marijuana. Mike helped himself to that when nobody was around. In homes where drug use is accepted young people grow up thinking that it is okay.

Parents don't have to drink with their children to give the message that it is okay. Parents who use drugs set the example that the way to deal with life is to use drugs. Remember, addiction runs in families. The social patterns in the family that support the dependence are just as strong.

The American society as a whole supports drug use. You see ads for beer and wine on TV. Music groups sing songs that make it sound cool to use drugs. On TV programs characters show that a drink before dinner is the way to go. When someone is upset, the good friend says, "You need a drink." The favorite meeting place in TV and movies is a bar. Jokes about drunks bring loud laughs. People wear T-shirts that say, "I don't have a drinking problem. I drink. I get drunk. I fall down. No problem."

Hiding a joint is just one of the sneaky ways teens fall into when they start to abuse drugs.

18   Americans like quick answers. What do you do when you have a headache? Take a pill. What do you do if you can't sleep? Take a spoonful of this. How do you lose weight? Take some of that. If you feel bad, smell bad, don't have a girlfriend, want a guy to notice you, want to have friends, what should you do? Take this pill. Use this soap. Try this toothpaste. Drink this beer. The message you get is that you should be perfect. You should never feel bad. You should be beautiful. You should have a girl or boyfriend.

Why do teens start using alcohol or another drug? It changes the way they feel. It helps them forget their problems. Too bad it makes those problems worse. It also gives them more problems. As problems get worse, they no longer feel good from the drugs. They must use more to feel less bad.

What makes drug use so appealing? The society you live in is a drug-using, plea-sure-seeking society. You get pressure to use drugs. Once the drug use starts, you don't know where it will go.

What started out for Rob as an adven-ture in the adult world became the night-mare of addiction. His good feelings are gone. He is a teenage addict.

CHAPTER 3

Teenage Addiction

*I*t hurts to admit it, but Lisa knows that her brother is a drug addict. It is as though she woke up one day and there he was, Rob the drug addict. The brother she knew and loved was gone. In his place was a monster she hated.

The change in Rob was not sudden. It didn't happen overnight. For a long time there were signs that Rob was getting into trouble. His disease progressed through four stages.

Stage I: Experimenting
From the time Rob was little his father gave him sips of beer. When he was in sixth grade, he and his friends sneaked

beer out of their houses. They drank it behind bushes in the park. All of them felt a little buzz. It was exciting because they knew they were not supposed to do it. Rob liked to feel high. He brought two cans most of the time.

When school started, he met lots of new kids. One of them asked him if he wanted to smoke *marijuana*. Wanting to be part of the group, Rob said yes. The marijuana made him feel even better than beer. He wanted to do it again.

Rob's period of experimenting was over. He began to go to parties where there was plenty of beer and pot. He crossed into the next stage of use.

Stage 2: Regular Use

Going to parties was lots of fun. It took four or five beers before Rob had a good buzz on. He was developing tolerance. Sometimes people had pills. There was always plenty of pot. Somebody might bring wine or a bottle of whiskey. Rob liked beer the best. He didn't like the hang-overs, but so what? He liked to party. He could drink a lot and still feel okay. He bragged about it and called others "light-weights." Sometimes Rob didn't remember

For the user, his supply is as near as the nearest phone—as long as he has the cash to pay for it.

what had happened the night before. He had blackouts.

Rob lied about where he was going and what he was doing. He had to be careful where he put his stash. He didn't want anyone to find it. He was always short of money, so he took money from his mother's purse. He started dealing drugs to pay for his own drugs.

It was hard to get home on time, so Rob's parents were always grounding him for being late. He told them they were picking on him. No one else's parents made such a big deal over being a little late. Of course, he didn't know what other parents did or said. He never went to anyone's house while parents were home.

Sometimes Rob stayed out all night. His parents really had a fit then. He told them he had stayed at a friend's house. He said he had not called home because he didn't want to wake them up. Lying was becoming a way of life for Rob.

Meeting his friends before school to get high made Rob late. He cut class sometimes and went to someone's house to drink beer or get high. He missed wrestling practice because he forgot or wanted to get high instead. Finally the coach cut him from the team. Rob didn't much care.

When old friends tried to talk to Rob about what was happening, he got mad. He told them to buzz off. Thinking about getting high was all he cared about. Rob was entering the next stage.

Stage 3: Harmful Involvement

Not yet chemically dependent, Rob was harmfully involved with drugs. Alcohol and marijuana were not enough. He tried anything that was around. He liked *speed* a lot. *Acid* and *PCP* were okay, but he didn't go looking for them. When he had the money, *cocaine* was his favorite.

Parties lasted all weekend. Most weekends Rob left home on Friday night and didn't get back until Sunday . If he came home Saturday, he slept all day.

By now, Rob was only interested in getting high. If he went to class, he was thrown out more often than not. He didn't care. School was a drag.

Home was a war zone. Rob's parents tried everything to make him shape up. It did no good. He got mad and took off for days. His sister Lisa was such a goody-goody that Rob couldn't stand her. His little brother Tommy was all right. When the door was locked, Tommy always opened his bedroom window for Rob.

The violence that often comes with drug use may cause siblings
to fear for their lives.

Rob stole the family silver and sold it
for drugs. He let his friends in to steal the
VCR. Anything of value disappeared from
the house. There still wasn't enough
money for the drugs Rob needed. His tolerance was so great that it took a lot to
make him high. He began "doing houses"
with some of his friends. They got caught,
but he didn't have to go to jail. It was his
first time, so he was given a court date and
sent home with his parents.

Rob's parents know that he does drugs.
He doesn't care anymore. He told them
there was nothing they could do about it.
What he did not tell them was that there's
nothing he can do about it either. He is
addicted. He can't stop doing drugs. He
doesn't like what is happening to him, but
he doesn't know what to do about it.

Stage 4: Chemical Dependence

At this point addicts don't use to feel good.
They use to feel less bad. They have to use
to feel normal. Many parents give up. The
only friends addicts have are their drug-
using buddies. They are often physically
ill. They get flu and colds easily. Their
lungs are weak from marijuana use. If they
smoke crack, they often cough up black

26 | mucus. They have no choice over their using. They must use because the need is so great.

The need for money keeps them doing things against the law. Drug dealing increases. Girls exchange sex for drugs or for money to buy drugs.

Addicts don't see that their drug use is causing them problems. They blame others for what is happening to them. Even if they question their use, their need is so great that they can't stop. They hate themselves and often think about suicide. They may want help, but many don't know how to get it. Some are lucky and ask for help or have people who get them to help. The unlucky ones die of their disease.

The time it takes to go from Stage 1 to the end of Stage 3 is different for each person. In some teens the progression is as fast as six months. Others might use for a year before getting into real trouble. Teens who use cocaine get into trouble within a couple of months. With crack cocaine, the addiction develops in a few weeks.

As the disease progresses in the teen, the family reacts to the unusual behavior. Family members develop their own form of the disease.

CHAPTER 4

Why Do My Parents Act This Way?

After Rob left, Lisa sat by the door crying for a long time. If only her parents would do something about Rob. Why did they always make excuses for him? They had to know that he was using drugs. Why didn't they do something?

Codependence of Parents

Living with a chemically dependent person affects the whole family. Those who are affected by someone else's dependency are called *codependents*. Codependents behave in unusual ways themselves. Your parents are under great stress. They are behaving in ways they don't understand. Your parents confuse you. They are often unreasonable. They are hard to get along with because of their illness of codependence. Their behavior may be much like that of Rob's parents. Pat and Jim Harris are reacting to Rob as most parents react to their teen's druggie behavior. They go through stages as their dependent children do.

Stages 1 and 2: Experimenting and Regular Use

During experimenting, not enough chemicals are used to change the teen's behavior. Parents don't notice any unusual behavior that makes them react. In the early stages of regular use, problems start to come up at school. Rob's mother got calls from teachers about his behavior in class. The attendance office called about his cutting class. Pat said she would talk to Rob. When teachers sent notices of Rob's poor work, she didn't tell her husband. She thought Jim would make too much of it. When Rob got three Ds on his report card, Pat did have to tell Jim about it. Rob complained that his teachers didn't like him. He made it sound as if they picked on him. Jim went to school and had Rob's classes changed.

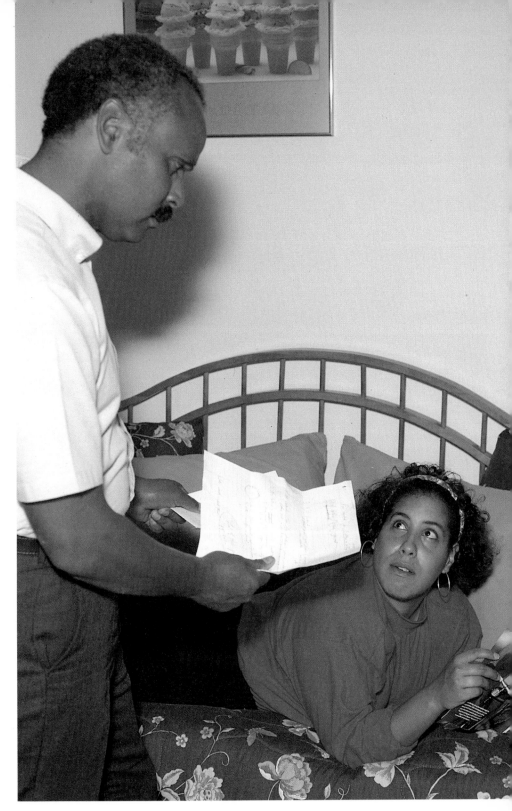

Falling grades and frequent truancy bring about angry family scenes.

Drinking and listening to the stereo can become a teenager's
way of life—even TV can seem too much trouble.

Like many parents, Pat and Jim had conferences with the teachers. They arranged for Rob to bring home progress reports every week. Rob brought the report home for two weeks. After that he always had an excuse for not having it. His parents soon knew that Rob was not going to bring the reports home no matter what they did. The more concerned they were, the less concerned Rob was.

Rob didn't do his jobs around the house. He was staying out late. It seemed to Pat that she was always nagging him about something. Both his parents were unhappy when Rob didn't want to go places with the family. He talked back all the time, especially to his mother. He was fighting more with Lisa and Tommy, too. When he wasn't fighting, Rob shut himself in his room and listened to his stereo. Pat was confused and hurt by his behavior. Jim was angry.

Stage 3: Harmful Involvement

As Rob got more into his drug use, Pat and Jim got more into trying to control him. It was important to them that Rob go to school. When school called to say that Rob missed classes, Pat made excuses for him. When he started skipping the whole day,

Wondering becomes certainty when a teenager finds drugs in her brother's jeans.

she still covered for him. She didn't want school to know that she didn't know where he was. Pat decided to make sure that Rob got to school. Every morning she got him up and drove him to school. Rob walked in the front door and out the back.

When his parents discovered that Rob was stealing from them, they asked him about it. He lied, of course. He told them they were terrible parents because they didn't trust him. Pat and Jim felt guilty.

When the arguments started to get worse, Pat and Jim tried all kinds of punishments. None worked. If they grounded him, Rob sneaked out the window after everyone went to bed. Jim called parents of Rob's friends to see if he was with them. He was shocked to find that none of them had seen Rob in months.

Pat knew that Rob smoked marijuana. She found it in his pants and shirt pockets when she washed his clothes. She didn't tell Jim about it. She didn't ask Rob about it. She was afraid he might be doing other drugs, too. She didn't want to know. It was too frightening even to think about.

Because they were so involved with Rob, the Harrises paid little attention to their other children. They snapped at Tommy and Lisa. Their shouting frightened

34 | Tommy. These were not the parents Lisa knew. Her parents were fighting with each other over Rob. The family was coming apart.

When the call came from the police that Rob had been arrested, Pat didn't know what to do. She told Jim that she thought Rob was using drugs.

When they saw Rob at the juvenile center, Jim got angry. He accused Rob of using drugs and said he had to stop. Rob shouted that he would do what he wanted. Nobody could make him stop using drugs.

Rob was given a date to appear in court and sent home with his parents. Whether or not the Harris family goes into Stage 4 depends on what they do now. Will they reach out for help for Rob and themselves? It is as close as the telephone. Who will make the move? If no one does, their disease of codependence will get worse along with Rob's disease of addiction.

Stage 4: Dependence

Many parents in the Harrises' position don't want their teen to go to jail. They hire lawyers and do all they can to keep the user out of jail. Then they expect the dependent to shape up and be grateful. But the behavior just gets worse.

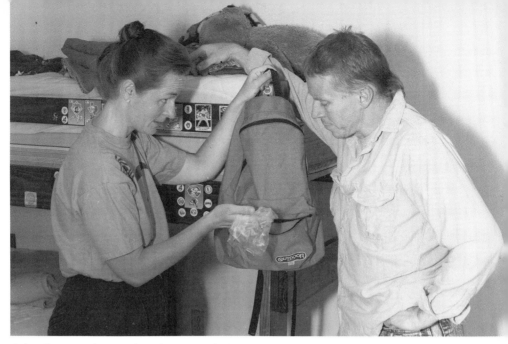

A family struggling with a drug user falls into verbal and physical violence.

Parents soon give up trying to get their drug-using teens to go to school. The fights get worse. Name-calling, cursing, and shouting get worse. Anger is so great that physical abuse is common. Users beat brothers and sisters. Boys frighten mothers so they can do as they please. Fathers get so angry they use their fists.

When the fighting gets bad, users often leave. They take off for days and weeks. The family is relieved, but the parents worry about the safety of the user.

Parents in Stage 4 feel hopeless and helpless. They feel that they have failed as parents and as people. Feelings of hatred for the user make them feel guilty. They think they are bad people. They feel responsible for the behavior of the user.

36 | Parents are supposed to be able to control their children. The schools and the courts tell them to do "something" about their children. No one tells them *how* to do "something" or *what* that "something" is.

It is not unusual for parents to throw teen addicts out of the house. They give up on them. Parents see that the whole family is suffering. They feel guilty because the other children have been hurt. They feel lost and helpless. Parents need support from people who understand. There are people in your community who can help.

Getting Help for the Family

Today there is treatment for teen addicts. There is also help for families of addicts. Treatment centers in your area advertise on TV. County agencies help teens and families in trouble with drugs. The National Council on Alcoholism often has people who can help you. Al-Anon groups are for families of alcoholics/addicts. Many cities have Al-Anon groups especially for parents. TOUGHLOVE Parent Support Groups help parents deal with teens in trouble. There is help for your parents in your community.

CHAPTER 5

What Is Happening to Me?

As she sat on the floor Lisa said over and over, "What is happening to me? What is going on?" She felt out of control and frightened. She didn't know what to do. Somehow she felt she should know what to do. It was very confusing.

Siblings (brothers and sisters) of drug users are codependent, too. Their codependence gets worse just as the disease of their sibling does. As the sibling of a drug user, you go through the same four stages of the disease.

Stages 1 and 2: Experimenting and Regular Use

Siblings of users often know when the drug use begins. A brother comes home

38 and brags about what a good time he had. A sister tells about the fun she had at a party. When Rob first talked about drinking beer and getting high, Lisa got a kind of thrill out of it. She was interested in knowing what it felt like to the high on marijuana. She didn't think much about Rob's drinking and using until his trouble at school started.

Although Lisa and Rob got along pretty well, they always had arguments. When the drug use started, the reasons for fighting changed. Rob was so touchy that he got mad over nothing. He started picking on Tommy too. That made Tommy try harder to please him. Rob was Tommy's big brother. Tommy looked up to him.

When Rob needed to get into the house at night, Tommy let him in. Lisa covered for Rob too. The more they covered for Rob, the worse his behavior became. By covering for Rob, they were *enablers*. As enablers they saved Rob from the bad things that would happen if his behavior was found out. They helped him to continue using and to progress to Stage 3.

Stage 3: Harmful Involvement

As Rob got more into his drug use, Lisa became more upset by his behavior. She

Keeping the secret of a sibling's drug abuse makes for a lonely life.

40 told him he was messing up. She wanted him to shape up. Rob told her to mind her own business.

Lisa could not tell her parents what was going on. She had covered for Rob for so long that she couldn't tell on him now. Her parents were hurting too much already. Besides, Lisa was afraid of what Rob might do if she told. As her parents looked for answers, Lisa knew what was causing the trouble. Cutting school to get high with druggie friends caused the failing grades. Breaking rules and fighting with the family were from using drugs. Lisa knew all that, but she didn't know what to do about it.

Poor Tommy was really in a spot. He knew almost all of Rob's secrets. When Rob took off for days, he got Tommy to bring him food and clothes. Tommy knew Rob's sleazy using friends. He knew where they took the goods they stole from houses. One time Rob's friends made Tommy smoke some marijuana. Rob didn't stop them. Tommy was scared, so he did what they wanted. Life was a nightmare for Tommy. He knew that Rob was doing something bad. He wanted his parents to stop Rob, but he couldn't tell them what Rob was doing. Confused and helpless, he kept covering for Rob. He loved Rob too much to do anything else.

Like Lisa and Tommy, you may be covering for a sibling. Your reason could be different. In many families brothers and sisters stick together because they don't get along with their parents. If that is the case, you side with the users. You cover for them, lie for them, and keep them out of trouble if you can.

Carrying that kind of secret weighs you down. You feel helpless and disloyal. If you tell on your siblings, you feel you betray them. By keeping the secret, you're disloyal to your parents.

Lisa and Tommy wanted their parents to do something about Rob. The yelling and fighting went nowhere. Rob just got worse. Their parents turned into people they didn't know. Nobody talked to anybody. Everybody hated everybody else. Lisa felt guilty because she hated Rob. Lately she even hated her parents. Good daughters don't hate their parents. Good sisters don't hate their brothers. Lisa was miserable and unhappy.

Tommy was confused and hated all the fighting. He wanted his parents to notice him, but they didn't. He tried being bad like Rob to get their attention. His mother

Sometimes running away seems like the only answer for a teenager in a family fighting over a sibling's drug abuse.

kept saying, "What's the matter with you? You know better than that." Tommy couldn't be bad enough to make his parents notice. Besides, he felt so guilty that he had to go back to being good. Sometimes he hated his parents for thinking only of Rob. He was angry because they didn't make Rob stop using drugs.

Sometimes children are hurt by older brothers and sisters. They are angry because their parents don't protect them from their addicted siblings. Child abuse is against the law no matter who does it. You deserve to be protected from that. Lisa deserves to be safe in her own home.

As she sat on the floor by the door, Lisa knew she had to do something. She had not meant to cross Rob today. Sometimes there was nothing she could do to avoid him. When Rob was coming off drugs and needed more, he was dangerous. She had to do something. Will that "something" help Lisa stop her disease from getting worse, or will it be a step into Stage 4?

Stage 4: Chemical Dependence
As parents give up on the user, so do the brothers and sisters. Those who are older leave home. They go away to school or move out on their own as soon as possible.

44 Younger siblings avoid the user. Much of the time they do that by playing and staying at friends' homes. Getting away is the most common behavior in Stage 4.

If your mother is a single mother, you may feel that protecting her from your using sibling is your job. Younger brothers and sisters often look to you for protection. That is especially true if parents seem powerless to do anything. If it happens to you, it tears you apart. You want to leave, yet you feel tied to the family by this huge responsibility. You are angry because it is put on you. But you feel guilty for wanting to get away. You are caught in the trap of codependence.

By the time you reach Stage 4, there is little left of the family. Everyone feels powerless and lost. No one wants to be part of the family. You just want someone to do something that will make it all better. You want someone to wave a magic wand, make your brother or sister well, and make all the hurt disappear.

Magic does not happen, but recovery does. There are things you can do to help your brother or sister. You can be the one to take the first step toward stopping the progression of the disease in your family.

CHAPTER 6

How Can I Help My Brother/ Sister?

It was at least a half hour since Lisa had heard the front door slam as Rob left the house. She got up and washed her face. Then she got the phone book. Opening it to the yellow pages, she turned to Drug Abuse. She dialed a number, and when someone answered, she said, "I think my brother is a drug addict. How can I help him?"

Ask for Help

When you don't know what to do, ask for help. You can't handle the problem alone. There are people who can help your family. A simple phone call can start help on

45

46 | the way. Lisa looked under Drug Abuse in the yellow pages. That is a good place to start. Your county health services often have alcohol and drug clinics. Ask how families of drug abusers can get help. More places to find help are in the Help List at the end of the book.

Stop Covering

If you have been covering for your brothers or sisters, STOP. By covering for them you make it easier for them to keep on using. Here are some of the things siblings do to "help" their brothers and sisters continue to use.

- Let them in when doors are locked.
- Don't tell when they break the rules.
- Lend them money.
- Don't tell when they steal from the family.
- Take food and clothes to them when they run away.
- Fight with them at every chance.
- Let them have their way so they won't get mad.
- Side with them against the parents.
- Do their school work for them.
- Pretend everything is fine.
- Don't tell that they're doing drugs.
  If you're doing any of these things, STOP. You are not helping.

What Can Help?

It is time to talk about all the secrets. Your parents need to know what is going on. If you cannot talk to your parents, talk to an adult you trust. That person can help you talk to your parents. If your school has a drug abuse counselor, talk to her or him. Working with families is an important part of that counselor's job.

Lisa looked for help from a treatment center. That is a good place to learn about chemical dependence. Treatment centers often have classes for families. They explain how to get someone like Rob to go for help. Someone there can help you talk to your parents.

The teenager with a drug addicted sibling needs most of all someone to talk to.

48   TOUGHLOVE Parent Support Groups help parents who don't know how to deal with troubled teenagers. If your town has a group, find out when it meets. Tell your parents about the group. TOUGHLOVE groups know about drug-using teens. They know what parents must do to get their teen drug abusers to help. Thousands of teens are off drugs today because their parents went to TOUGHLOVE.

Your other brothers and sisters need to know about the disease of chemical dependence. They need to understand that the drug user in your family is very ill. They need to know that the whole family has this illness. It is important for them to know that everyone in the family needs help. You can tell them about help that is found for the family. Most of all, you can talk to them about what is happening to them. You can listen to their feelings and their fears. You can share your feelings and fears. You can support them when they talk to your parents.

Not all families are willing to get help. Your parents may not want to hear what you have to say. The rest of the family may not understand what you want to do. Even if the disease is not stopped in the rest of your family, you can get help yourself.

CHAPTER 7

How Can I Help Myself?

*A*s she walked down the hall after support group, Lisa felt she wasn't alone any more. It was two weeks since she had made the phone call to the drug abuse treatment center. The woman there had told her about her school's chemical dependency counselor. Lisa had gone to see Ms. Sellers at school. Ms. Sellers had invited her to the support group for students worried about someone else's drinking or drug use. Lisa was surprised to see brothers and sisters of some of Rob's druggie friends. When the group started sharing, Lisa heard her own story over and over. The others had the same fears and hurts. Lisa felt listened to and understood. She felt part of the group. She wasn't alone.

50 *Helping Yourself*

Get Support

The best way to help yourself is to get help from others. Lisa is lucky. She has a support group right in her school. Many schools have Student Assistance Programs. Check it out in your school. Ask your school counselor or school nurse about Alateen. Alateen is a support group for teens who are affected by someone else's drinking or using.

Talk to an adult you trust. You need someone older who can be there for you. If your town has a TOUGHLOVE Parent Support Group, call and ask for help. Many parents in those groups understand how it is for you. They can listen and help you to change your codependent behavior.

Don't Blame Yourself or Others

Many siblings of users think that something they do causes their brothers and sisters to use. Lisa thought that fighting with Rob made him go out and use. In group she learned about the three Cs. You didn't CAUSE the drug use. You can't CONTROL it. You can't CURE it. The same is true of your parents or your sibling's friends. No one is to blame.

A teenager with an addicted sibling needs to get out and make a life for herself.

52 | Don't Withdraw from Others

Going to the same school with a druggie brother or sister is tough. You think everyone sees you the way they do your sibling. When teachers hear your last name, they look at you as if to say, "Oh no, not another one." Just remember, you are not your brother. What your sister or brother does is not you. Be part of school activities. Don't stay away from people because you're afraid they think you're like your brother or sister. You need other people in your life. Having interests outside your home is important. Get your mind off what is wrong and on what is right. What is right is taking part in activities that you enjoy. Don't worry about what people think of your sibling. They will see you for who you are.

Don't Take Things Personally

When your brothers or sisters yell and call you names, try not to get upset. They are not in their right mind. Stop thinking, "Why is she doing this to me?" She isn't doing it to you personally. She steals your money. She would steal anyone's money. Her disease tells her to take what she needs. It does no good to get mad at her. Get mad at the disease.

Don't Drink or Use Drugs Yourself

Your chances of becoming chemically dependent are very high. Drinking or using will not help your problems. It will just give you more problems. Many addicted teens think it is fun to get their brothers and sisters loaded. They want a using buddy in the house. Don't get caught in their trap.

Make Sure You are Safe

If your sibling is violent, make sure you are safe. Leave the house if it is possible. Go to a neighbor's house. If you feel un-comfortable going to a neighbor's house, GO ANYWAY. Stay with a friend. GET TO A SAFE PLACE. If you fear for your safety, CALL THE POLICE. Don't worry about how angry your parents will be. CALL THE POLICE. Don't take chances with someone who is drugged. Your personal safety is the most important thing.

Be Good to Yourself

The disease of chemical dependence robs you of feeling good about yourself. It makes you feel that something is wrong with you. It is time for you to tell yourself how good you are instead of how bad you are. Look in the mirror every day and tell

54 yourself how good you are. Here are some ways to do that.

I am a good person.
I like myself.
I am lovable.
I am worthwhile.
I am important.
I deserve to be happy.
I am special.
I deserve good things.
It's okay if I'm not perfect.
I respect myself.
I am the best me I can be.
I am a caring person.

You may not feel too comfortable doing that at first. Keep at it. You'll soon grow to like it. What is even better—you will believe it.

Helping yourself is something you need help with. You can't deal with this disease alone. You don't have to. Reach out to those who are waiting to help you. Stop being part of the problem. Become part of the solution.

Fact Sheet

- In a 1989 survey of high school seniors:
    35.4% used an illegal hard drug in the
      last year.
    19.7% used an illegal drug in the last 30
      days.
    43.7% used marijuana in the last year.
    33% are heavy drinkers.

- 50:9% of high school seniors will try an
  illegal drug before graduation.

- Alcohol is the drug most used by teens
  today.

- There are 3.5 million teenage alcoholics.

- Alcohol and other drugs are the cause of
  60% of the deaths on American highways.

- Every 20 minutes someone dies because of
  a drunk driver.

- Each year 9,500 young people under 25 die because of drinking drivers.

- Drinking drivers kill 350 youths under 15 and injure over 12,000 every year.

- 60% of all crime is drug related.
- Drug use is higher among those who have not completed high school.

- Marijuana and cocaine use is twice as high in students who cut class four or more times.

- The U.S. uses over 60% of the cocaine that is produced.

- 93% of all people who have tried cocaine used marijuana first.

- Marijuana causes short-term memory loss for at least six weeks after use is stopped.

- Today's marijuana is ten to twelve times stronger than the marijuana of the 1960s.

Glossary
Explaining New Words

acid Street name for the hallucinogen LSD.

addiction The compulsion to use a drug, with loss of control and continued use no matter what happens to you or others.

Al-Anon A community group of people who are affected by someone else's alcohol (and other drug) use. They meet and share feelings and help one another deal with problems.

Alateen A community group of young people who are affected by someone else's alcohol (and other drug) use. They meet to share feelings and help one another deal with problems.

Alcoholics Anonymous (AA) A community group of chemically dependent people who meet to share feelings and help one another to stay well and not drink or use other drugs.

alcoholism An illness that causes people to become dependent on alcohol because of changes in the brain.

blackout No memory of what went on while drinking or using other drugs.

chemical dependence A strong feeling of need for a drug that causes people to keep taking the drug even when it is harmful.

cocaine A powerful central nervous system stimulant taken from the leaves of the coca plant and made into a powder that is sniffed, smoked, or injected.

Cocaine Anonymous (CA) A community group of cocaine addicts who meet to share feelings and help one another to stay well and not use cocaine or other drugs.

codependent Someone affected by another person's chemical dependence.

compulsion Uncontrolled need to do something again and again.

denial Unwillingness to admit the truth; unwillingness to admit there is a problem with chemicals.

depression A feeling of deep sadness; feeling "down."

drug A chemical substance that changes how the mind or body functions.

enable To cover for the dependent so s/he does not experience the harmful effects of her/his behavior; to make it easier for someone to continue using drugs.

illegal Against the law.

joint Marijuana cigarette.

PCP A strong hallucinogen.

peer Someone your own age.

physical Having to do with the body.

pot Street name for marijuana.

prescription drugs Medicines that must be ordered by a doctor and prepared by a pharmacist.

progression Movement through stages.

psychological Having to do with the mind.

speed Street name for amphetamines; also called uppers, pep pills, bennies, exies, meth, crystal, crank.

stash drug supply.

tolerance Needing more of the drug to get the same effect.

withdrawal Cramps, fever, chills, shaking, and upset stomach that happen when drugs are stopped; the feeling of anxiety, fear, and confusion that happens when drugs are stopped.

Help List

Telephone Book

Yellow Pages
- Alcoholism, Drug Abuse, Counselors

White Pages
- Alcoholics Anonymous, Al-Anon, Narcotics Anonymous, National Council of Alcoholism, Alcoholism, Counseling, Drug Abuse Services, Cocaine Anonymous, Alateen (Call Al-Anon and ask about Alateen)

Government Listings
- Alcoholism Treatment, Drug Abuse, County Health Services

Write or Call

- National Association of Children of Alcoholics
  31706 Pacific Coast Highway, Suite 20
  South Laguna, CA 95677
- National Council on Alcoholism
  12 West 21st Street
  New York, NY 10010
  (212) 206-6770
- Alcoholics Anonymous World Services, Inc.
  P.O. Box 459, Grand Central Station
  New York, NY 10163

- Al-Anon Family Group Headquarters
  P.O. Box 1782, Madison Square Station
  New York, NY 10159

- Narcotics Anonymous
  World Service Office
  16155 Wyandotte Street
  Van Nuys, CA 91406
- TOUGHLOVE
  P.O. Box 1069
  Doylestown, PA 18901

Hot Lines

- 800-Cocaine   Answers any questions
  about cocaine.
- 800-67PRIDE   For information about
  alcohol/drugs.

Check the bulletin boards in the school nurse's office and counseling office for TEEN HOT LINES in your town.

Places That Have Support Groups

- Your city's National Council on Alcoholism
- County Mental Health Services
- County Juvenile Services
- Your School Counseling Office
- Your School Nurse
- Teen Clinic

For Further Reading

Not Hard to Read

Hull-Mast, Nancy, and Purcell, Diane. *Sibs: The Forgotten Family Members.* Park Ridge, IL: Parkside Publishing, 1989.

Taylor, Barbara. *Everything You Need to Know about Alcohol.* New York: The Rosen Publishing Group, 1989.

Twist, Clint. *The Crack and Cocaine Epidemic.* New York: Franklin.

Not So Easy to Read
But Worth Looking At

Edwards, Gabrielle I. *Coping with Drug Abuse,* rev. ed. New York: The Rosen Publishing Group, 1990.

McFarland, Rhoda. *Coping with Substance Abuse,* rev. ed. New York: The Rosen Publishing Group, 1990.

Scott, Sharon. *How to Say No and Keep Your Friends.* Amherst, MA: Human Resource Development Press, Inc., 1986.

Index

About the Author

Rhoda McFarland has taught all grades kindergarten through twelfth. She is a certified alcoholism and drug abuse counselor having worked with troubled young people and their parents. She developed and implemented the first educational program in the California area for students making the transition from drug/alcohol treatment programs back into the regular school system. She is currently working as a Peace Corps volunteer in Belize, Central America.

Photo Credits

Cover photo: Chuck Peterson
Photos on pages 2, 6, 12, 17, 21, 24, 30, 32, 39: Michael F. O'Brien; pages 29, 35, 42, 51: Stuart Rabinowitz; page 47: Chris Volpe

Design & Production: Blackbirch Graphics, Inc.